Stonewall Jackson

MILITARY LEADERS OF THE CIVIL WAR

Don McLeese

Rourke
Publishing LLC
Vero Beach, Florida 32964

www.rourkepublishing.com

PHOTO CREDITS: Title Page ©PhotoDisc, Inc.
P10, P 18/19, P21 Courtesy of the Virginia Military Institute Archives
all other images from the Library of Congress

Title page: Part of a large carving at Stone Mountain, Georgia, showing (from left to right) Robert E. Lee and Stonewall Jackson.

Editor: Frank Sloan

Cover and page design by Nicola Stratford

Library of Congress Cataloging-in-Publication Data

McLeese, Don.
  Stonewall Jackson / Don McLeese.
    p. cm. -- (Military leaders of the civil war)
  Includes index.
  ISBN 1-59515-477-9 (hardcover)
  1. Jackson, Stonewall, 1824-1863--Juvenile literature. 2. Generals--Confederate States of America--Biography--Juvenile literature. 3. Confederate States of America. Army--Biography--Juvenile literature. 4. United States--History--Civil War, 1861-1865--Campaigns--Juvenile literature. I. Title.
  E467.1.J15M28 2006
  973.7'42'092--dc22

                              2005010981

Printed in the USA

Rourke Publishing
1-800-394-7055
www.rourkepublishing.com
sales@rourkepublishing.com
Post Office Box 3328, Vero Beach, FL 32964

Table of Contents

~

The Man Called Stonewall

Except for Robert E. Lee, the head of the **Confederate** army, no Southern **general** was better known or more respected than Thomas Jackson.

He earned his nickname, "Stonewall," in 1861, at the First Battle of Bull Run. Jackson's Confederate side had only 17,000 **soldiers** to fight more than 60,000 on the Union side. Jackson refused to give ground, and his Southern soldiers defeated the Northern soldiers.

Another Southern general saw Jackson and his **troops** refusing to run away and said, "There is Jackson standing like a stone wall." The name stuck. From that time on, General Thomas Jackson would always be known as Stonewall Jackson.

4

Jackson was such an important leader of the Southern army that Robert E. Lee called him "my right arm."

Stonewall Jackson's birthplace in Clarksburg, West Virginia

An Orphan Boy

~

Thomas Jonathan Jackson was born on January 21, 1824, in Clarksburg, Virginia. (This town became a part of West Virginia during the Civil War.) Tom's father was a lawyer. He died when Tom was two. Tom's mother died when he was six. From that time on, Tom was an **orphan**.

When his mother became sick, Tom was sent to live with his uncle, Cummins Jackson, the brother of his father. Tom had been too young when his father died to remember much about him but he loved his mother very much and missed her a lot. He would think of his early childhood as very sad.

West Virginia: West Virginia was part of Virginia until the Civil War. It didn't become its own state until 1863.

Life on the Farm

~

Tom's uncle lived on a large farm called Jackson's Mill, near what is now Weston, West Virginia. Many of the boy's other uncles and aunts lived and worked there as well.

The farm had a sawmill where trees were turned into wood for building. It also had a grain mill that turned the crops grown on the farm into grains for cooking. There were horses on the farm, and Tom loved to ride and race them.

Mills: In the days before electricity or gas power, many mills got their power from the current of moving water. They were often located in a building by a river or a creek. Another type of mill, called a windmill, gets its energy from the wind.

Jackson's boyhood home near Weston, West Virginia

A photograph of Thomas Jackson about the time he went to West Point

School Days

~

When Tom was growing up, most farm boys had little opportunity to go to school. They were supposed to work on the farm, which didn't leave much time. Tom only went to school for a few months a year. But he was such a smart student that he was made a teacher at the local school when he was only 16.

Country schools: Most country schools back then had just one classroom, and students of all ages studied together. Working the farm was more important than going to school.

West Point

~

By the time Tom turned 18, he knew he had to have more schooling or he would spend his life on the farm. He became interested in the U.S. **Military** Academy in West Point, New York. The college gave students a good education and trained them to be officers in the army. Best of all, it was free!

Tom needed a letter from his **congressman** saying that he deserved to go to West Point. A congressman could only recommend one student. Though Tom hadn't gone to school very much, his family and neighbors all wrote to the congressman to tell him what a fine young man Tom was. He would make a good student and officer. It was one of the biggest days in Tom's young life when he learned in 1842 that West Point would admit him.

12

*A view of the Hudson River with the U.S. Military Academy
at West Point on the cliffs at the left*

*Young soldiers were taught how to fight battles
on horseback and how to use weapons.*

Graduation

~

Most of those who came to West Point had more schooling than Tom did. He had to study a lot harder to keep up. But Tom had always been willing to work hard. He didn't do as well on early tests as other students, but he did better as he went along.

In addition to studying school subjects such as math, science, and history, Tom learned how to be a good soldier.

By the time Tom graduated in 1846, he was in the top third of his class. Other students said that if school had lasted one more year, Tom would have been first in his class! After graduating, he joined the army, where he was given the rank of second **lieutenant**.

15

Military ranks: Members of the army obey the orders of those who rank above them. General is the top rank. Private is the lowest rank. Other ranks include sergeant, major, and lieutenant.

Off to War!

~

Very quickly, Tom and many of the others who had been at West Point with him were sent to Mexico. The United States and Mexico were fighting about the border between the two countries. At the time, much of what is now the American Southwest was still under Mexican control, as was what is now California.

Tom fought in many battles and was very brave. He became a war hero. He was with the American army when it entered Mexico City in September, 1847, and won the war. After the war, he was honored with new ranks: first lieutenant and then major.

The Mexican War: This lasted from 1846 to 1848. At the end, America gained more than a half-million square miles of land that used to belong to Mexico and paid Mexico $15 million for the land.

16

In 1846, after Mexican soldiers crossed into Texas, the United States declared war on Mexico.

Young Thomas Jackson

A Man of God

~

Tom was known not only as one of the best and bravest of military leaders, but also as one of the most religious. He joined the Presbyterian Church and spent a lot of time reading the Bible. One of the reasons that Tom was so brave was because he had faith that God would take care of him.

A religious man, Jackson often said prayers with his troops before going into battle.

Leaving the Army

~

In 1851, Tom left the army to become a teacher. He taught for ten years at the Virginia Military Academy, where his students wanted to become soldiers. He got married twice during that time. His first wife, Elinor Junkin, died the year after their marriage in 1853. In 1857, he married Mary Anna Morrison, the daughter of a Presbyterian minister.

A photograph of Jackson's second wife, Mary Anna Morrison

Union and Confederate forces met at Cedar Mountain,
in the Second Battle of Bull Run in August of 1862.

Civil War

~

When the Southern states wanted to leave the United States and form their own country, Tom didn't agree with this decision. He thought the United States should remain one country. But when Virginia decided to leave the United States to become one of the Confederate States of America, Tom was loyal to his state. In 1861, he joined the Confederate army, where he became one of its greatest generals.

The War Between the States: Another name for the Civil War. It lasted from 1861 until 1865, when the Confederate Army of the South surrendered to the Union Army of the North.

From Tom to Stonewall

~

Tom Jackson had long been a great military leader, but it was the First Battle of Bull Run in 1861 that made him famous as "Stonewall." He was the general who stood firm, who wouldn't allow his troops to retreat. He won the battle.

Over the next year, Stonewall Jackson continued to lead his outnumbered Southern troops in a series of famous battles, including the Second Battle of Bull Run.

He defended the Shenandoah Valley, which is 150 miles (241 km) from north to south. It was also an important supplier of food to the Confederates. Though the Union had more soldiers, Stonewall Jackson and the Southern forces kept control of the valley, in one of the greatest military **campaigns** in history.

24

Bull Run: This is the name of the creek near the town of Manassas, where two major battles were fought. Sometimes these are called the First and Second battles of Manassas.

A fierce fight ensues between North and South in the Second Battle of Bull Run.

A monument marks the spot where Jackson was shot.

Shot by Accident

On May 2, 1863, Stonewall Jackson and his soldiers were in a battle near Chancellorsville, Virginia. That night, the brave Stonewall went into enemy territory to scout. One of the Southern soldiers thought he saw a Northern soldier and shot him. Stonewall never recovered from the accidental shooting, and he died eight days later, on May 10.

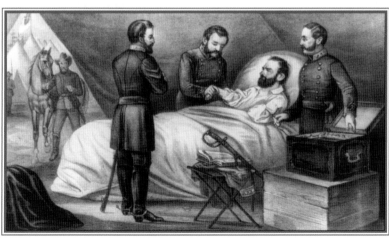

Stonewall Jackson on his deathbed

Robert E. Lee visits the grave of Stonewall Jackson.

"My Right Arm"

~

Before Stonewall died, his left arm became infected and needed to be **amputated**. The head of the Confederate Army, General Robert E. Lee, said of Jackson, "He has lost his left arm, but I have lost my right arm." When Stonewall Jackson died, the South lost one of its greatest military leaders.

Important Dates to Remember

1824   Thomas Jonathan Jackson is born.

1830   Orphan Tom moves to Jackson's Mill to live with his uncle.

1842   West Point admits Tom.

1846   Tom graduates from West Point and joins the army to fight in the Mexican-American War.

1851   Tom leaves the army to become a teacher.

1861   Tom joins the Confederate Army to fight the Civil War, earns the nickname "Stonewall" at Bull Run.

1862   Stonewall leads the Shenandoah Valley campaign.

1863   Stonewall Jackson dies after an accidental shooting.

Glossary

amputated (AM pew tayt ud) — cut off, removed by surgery

campaigns (kam PAINZ) — connected series of military battles or operations

Confederate (kon FED ur et) — a person, state, or soldier on the Southern side in the Civil War

congressman (KON gress man) — a member of congress (back then, they were all men)

general (JEN ur ul) — the highest rank in the military

lieutenant (loo TEN unt) — a military rank

military (MILL ih TARE ee) — the armed forces

orphan (OR fen) — a child whose mother and father are both dead

soldiers (SOHL jerz) — people who serve in the military

troops (TRUUPS) — soldiers

Index

Further Reading

Hewson, Martha. *Stonewall Jackson* (Famous Figures of the Civil War Era), Chelsea House, 2001.

Hughes, Christopher. *Stonewall Jackson* (Triangle Histories—the Civil War), Blackbirch Press, 2001.

Robertson, James I. *Standing Like a Stone Wall: The Life of Thomas J. Jackson*, Atheneum, 2001.

Websites To Visit

http://www.civilwarhistory.com/stonewalljackson/jackson.htm
http://www.vmi.edu/archives/jackson/tjjfaq.html
http://www.sonofthesouth.net/leefoundation/Stonewall_Jackson.htm

About The Author

Don McLeese is an associate professor of journalism at the University of Iowa. He has won many awards for his journalism, and his work has appeared in numerous newspapers and magazines. He has frequently contributed to the World Book Encyclopedia and has written many books for young readers. He lives with his wife and two daughters in West Des Moines, Iowa.